Enjoy Playing Guitar

T0057035

Christmas Crackers

14 easy arrangements with flexible accompaniments

Debbie Cracknell

MUSIC DEPARTMENT

OXFORD
UNIVERSITY PRESS

OXFORD
UNIVERSITY PRESS

Great Clarendon Street, Oxford OX2 6DP,
United Kingdom

Oxford University Press is a department of the University of Oxford.
It furthers the University's objective of excellence in research, scholarship,
and education by publishing worldwide. Oxford is a registered trade mark of
Oxford University Press in the UK and in certain other countries

© Oxford University Press 2015

Debbie Cracknell has asserted her right under the Copyright, Designs
and Patents Act, 1988, to be identified as the Arranger of these Works

Database right Oxford University Press (maker)

First published 2015

Impression: 1

All rights reserved. No part of this publication may be reproduced,
stored in a retrieval system, or transmitted, in any form or by any means,
without the prior permission in writing of Oxford University Press

Permission to perform this work in public (except in the course of divine
worship) should normally be obtained from the Performing Right Society Ltd
(PRS) at www.prsformusic.com or a local performing right licensing
organization, unless the owner or the occupier of the premises being used
already holds a licence from such an organization. Likewise, permission to
make and exploit a recording must be obtained in advance from the
Mechanical-Copyright Protection Society Ltd (MCPS) at www.prsformusic.com
or a local mechanical copyright licensing organization

Enquiries concerning reproduction outside the scope of the above
should be directed to the Music Rights Department, Oxford University Press,
at music.permission.uk@oup.com or at the address above

ISBN 978–0–19–340716–9

Music and text origination by Katie Johnston
Printed in Great Britain on acid-free paper by
Halstan & Co. Ltd., Amersham, Bucks.

Christmas Crackers

Frosty the snowman	4
Away in a manger	6
Deck the hall	8
Let it snow!	10
Once in royal David's city	12
In dulci jubilo	14
The Virgin Mary had a baby boy	16
We wish you a merry Christmas	18
Rockin' around the Christmas tree	20
Hark! the herald-angels sing	22
Jingle, Bells	24
Santa Claus is Comin' to Town	26
O little town of Bethlehem	28
Sleigh Ride	29
Chords	32

How to use this book

A versatile resource, this collection includes the melodies and words to your favourite Christmas pieces plus accompaniment options for all occasions. Developing guitarists can play the carol or song as a solo, as part of a duet with the bass part or strummed chords, or as part of a quartet or larger ensemble. The collection can also be used to accompany singers, in which case players should consider using capos to take the tune to a comfortable pitch. Bracketed dynamics show those to be followed on repeats.

The MELODY and ACCOMPANIMENT Parts 2 and 3 can be played by elementary level guitarists (approximately Grades 1–3). ACCOMPANIMENT Part 1 is easier still and can be played by near beginners; the note-knowledge required for this part is shown at the start of each score.

For guitarists more used to acoustic styles, there are chord symbols above the ACCOMPANIMENT scores and a corresponding table of chord boxes on page 32. And if that isn't enough, try adding percussion—sleigh bells in 'Jingle, Bells' (four-bar intro and from bar 21) and 'Sleigh Ride' (bars 17–32 and coda), or maracas in 'The Virgin Mary had a baby boy'. Many of the pieces can be extended through creating introductions based on the first or last few bars.

Here's wishing you a fun-filled Christmas play-along!

Frosty the snowman

Words by Walter E. 'Jack' Rollins
Music by Steve Nelson

MELODY

© 1950 (renewed) Chappell & Co. Inc., USA. This arrangement © 2015 Chappell & Co. Inc., USA (Warner Chappell North America Ltd). Reproduced by permission of Faber Music Ltd and Alfred Music Publishing Co. All rights reserved.

ACCOMPANIMENT

• Part 1 uses G, A, B, C, C♯, and D on strings 2 and 3.

Away in a manger

Words 19th-cent. American
Music by W. J. Kirkpatrick

MELODY

Tranquillo

mp (*repeat tasto*)

A - way in a___ man - ger, no___ crib for a bed, The___
cat - tle are___ low - ing, the___ ba - by a - wakes, But___

5

lit - tle Lord Je - sus laid___ down his sweet head; The
lit - tle Lord Je - sus no___ cry - ing he makes. I

9

stars in the___ bright sky looked down where he lay, The___
love thee, Lord___ Je - sus! Look___ down from the sky, And___

13

(**rit.**)

lit - tle Lord Je - sus a - sleep in the hay. The nigh.
stay by my side un - til___ morn - ing is

tasto = play over the fingerboard

© Oxford University Press 2015. Photocopying this copyright material is ILLEGAL.

ACCOMPANIMENT

• Part 1 uses B, C, D, and E on strings 1 and 2.

tasto = play over the fingerboard

Deck the hall

Welsh trad.

MELODY

Briskly, in 2

f

Deck the hall with boughs of hol - ly, Fa la la la la, fa la la la;
Fast a-way the old year pass - es, Fa la la la la, fa la la la;

5

'Tis the sea - son to be jol - ly, Fa la la la la, fa la la la.
Hail the new, ye lads and las - ses, Fa la la la la, fa la la la.

9

Fill the mead cup, drain the bar - rel, Fa la la la la la la la la;
Laugh - ing, quaff - ing, all to-geth - er, Fa la la la la la la la la;

13

Troll the an - cient Christ-mas ca - rol, Fa la la la la, fa la la la.
Heed - less of the wind and wea - ther, Fa la la la la, fa la la la.

© Oxford University Press 2015. Photocopying this copyright material is ILLEGAL.

ACCOMPANIMENT

- Part 1 uses D, E, and F on string 4.
- Part 2 is a descant—only play this part on the repeat.

Let it snow!

Words by Sammy Cahn
Music by Jule Styne

MELODY

'Let it snow! Let it snow! Let it snow!' © 1945 (renewed) Producers Music Publishing Co. Inc. and Cahn Music Co. This arrangement © 2015 Producers Music Publishing Co. Inc. and Cahn Music Co. All rights for Producers Music Publishing Co. Inc. administered by Chappell & Co. Inc. All rights for Cahn Music Co. administered by Imagem Sounds. Reproduced by permission of Hal Leonard Corporation, Faber Music Ltd, Alfred Music Publishing Co., and Music Sales Ltd. All rights reserved.

ACCOMPANIMENT

• Part 1 uses G, A, B, C, C♯, and D on strings 2 and 3.

Once in royal David's city

Words by C. F. Alexander
Music by H. J. Gauntlett

MELODY

© Oxford University Press 2015. Photocopying this copyright material is ILLEGAL.

ACCOMPANIMENT

• Part 1 uses G, B, C, and E on strings 1, 2, and 3.

In dulci jubilo

(*In sweet rejoicing*)

Old German carol

MELODY

ACCOMPANIMENT

- Part 1 uses G, A, and B on strings 2 and 3 and octave harmonics on strings 3 and 4.
- When playing the repeat, the harmonic section could be played again to form a link passage. Otherwise, repeat from the upbeat to bar 5.

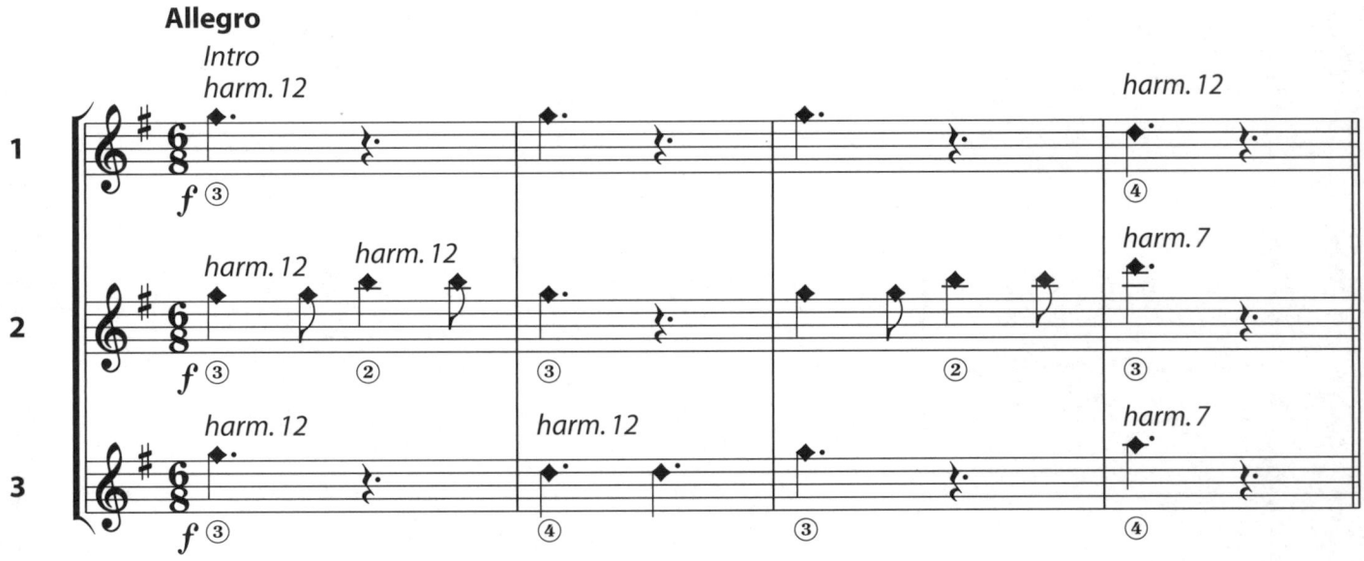

© Oxford University Press 2015. Photocopying this copyright material is ILLEGAL.

5
G
D7
mf
p
i
m
i
mf
mf
9
G
D7
G
13
D7
G
D7
G
17
C
D7
G
D7
1
G
2
G
rit.
harm. 12
harm. 12

The Virgin Mary had a baby boy

MELODY

West Indian trad.

Allegretto

Intro 3

The Vir - gin Ma - ry had a ba - by boy,_ the

7

Vir - gin Ma - ry had a ba-by boy,_ the Vir - gin Ma - ry had a ba-by boy, and they

11

say that his name was Je - sus. He come from the glo - ry,__ he come from the

16

glo - ri - ous king-dom. He come from the glo - ry,__ he come from the

20

glo - ri - ous king-dom. Oh yes, be-liev - er! Oh yes, be-liev - er!

25

Outro 4

He come from the glo - ry,__ he come from the glo-ri-ous king-dom.

ACCOMPANIMENT

• Part 1 uses G, B, C, D, E, F, and high G on strings 1, 2, and 3.

Allegretto

Intro

C G7 G C

1

2

3

*Tap on the body of the guitar, above the strings with the thumb and then below the strings with the fingers.

© Oxford University Press 2015. Photocopying this copyright material is ILLEGAL.

5
G
G7
C
C7
p i m p i m p i
10
F
C
G
C
C
Dm7
G7
p i m i p i m i
mf
15 (19)
C
F
G
C
F
C
F
p i m p i m p i
p i m i p i m i
24
C
Dm7
G7
C
F
G
C
mf
29
Outro
G7
G
C

We wish you a merry Christmas

MELODY

English trad.

ACCOMPANIMENT

• Part 1 uses B, C, D, E, and F on strings 1 and 2.

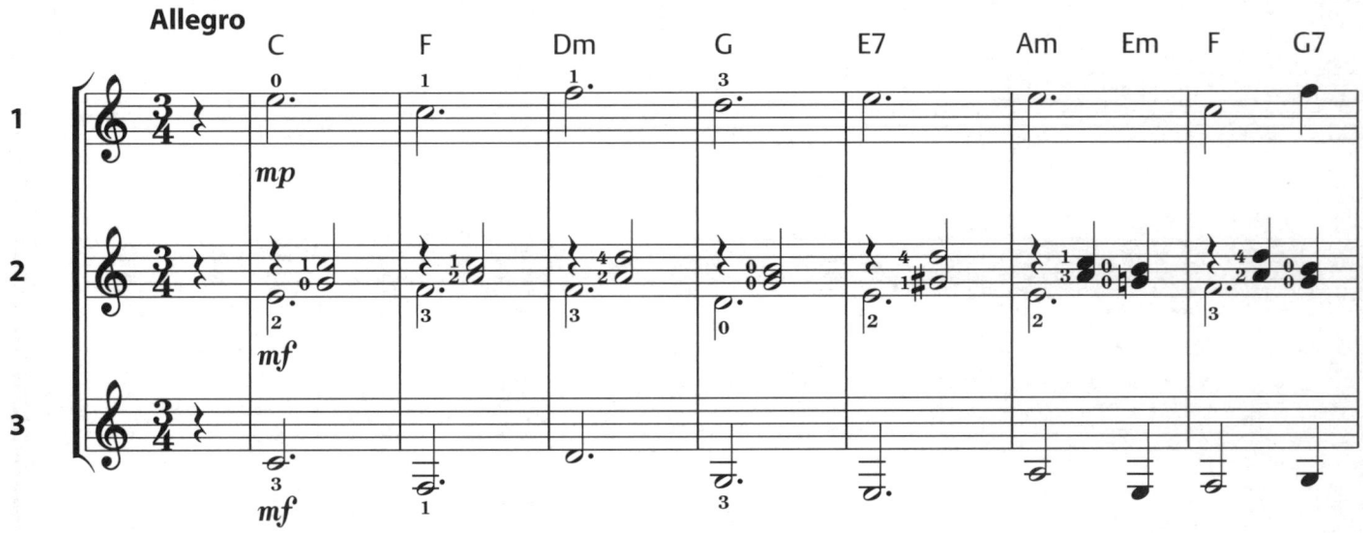

© Oxford University Press 2015. Photocopying this copyright material is ILLEGAL.

8
C
G
C
G
D7
G
C
Em
mf
f
f
15
F
G7
C
F
Dm
G
G7
p
cresc.
mp
cresc.
mp
cresc.
21
E7
Am
Em
F
G7
C
G
mp
mf
mf
27
C
G
D7
G
C
Em
F
G7
C
rit.
mf
f
f

Rockin' around the Christmas tree

Words and music by
Johnny Marks

MELODY

Moderato (♩♫ = ♩³♪)

mf

Rock-in' a - round the Christ-mas tree_ At the Christ-mas par - ty hop,___

5

Mis-tle-toe hung where you can see,_ ev - 'ry cou - ple tries to stop.

9

Rock-in' a - round the Christ-mas tree,_ Let the Christ-mas spi - rit ring,___

13

Lat - er we'll have some pump - kin pie,_ And we'll do some ca - rol - ing.

17

f II

You will get a sen - ti - men - tal feel - ing when you hear Voi - ces sing - ing,

22

IV II I *mf*

'Let's be jol - ly, Deck the halls with boughs of hol - ly'. Rock-in' a - round the

26

Christ - mas tree,_ Have a hap - py ho - li - day,___ Ev' - ry - one danc - ing

30

cresc. IV *f*

mer - ri - ly,___ In the new old - fash - ioned way.___

© 1961 Saint Nicholas Music Inc., USA. This arrangement © 2015 Saint Nicholas Music Inc., USA and Chappell Music Ltd, London.
Reproduced by permission of Faber Music Ltd. and Saint Nicholas Music Inc., USA. All rights reserved.

ACCOMPANIMENT

• Part 1 uses C♯, D, D♯, and E on strings 1 and 2.

Hark! the herald-angels sing

Words by Charles Wesley and others
Music by Felix Mendelssohn

MELODY

Moderato

mf

Hark! the he - rald - an - gels sing___ Glo - ry to the new - born King;

5

Peace on earth and mer - cy mild,___ God and sin - ners re - con - ciled:

9

III
1

Joy - ful all ye na - tions rise,___ Join the tri - umph of the skies,___

13

3 1 I 1

With th'an - gel - ic host pro - claim, Christ is___ born in Beth - le - hem.

III
17 *f*

I

Hark! the he - rald - an - gels sing Glo - ry___ to the new - born King.

© Oxford University Press 2015. Photocopying this copyright material is ILLEGAL.

ACCOMPANIMENT

• Part 1 uses G, A, B, C, and D on strings 2 and 3.

Jingle, Bells

Words and music by
J. Pierpont

MELODY

© Oxford University Press 2015. Photocopying this copyright material is ILLEGAL.

ACCOMPANIMENT

• Part 1 uses C, D, E, and F on strings 1 and 2.

Santa Claus is Comin' to Town

Words by Haven Gillespie
Music by J. Fred Coots

MELODY

Moderato (♩♫ = ♩³♪)

f

You bet - ter watch out, you bet - ter not cry, Bet - ter not pout, I'm
mak-ing a list and check-ing it twice, Gon - na find out who's

4

tell - ing you why: San - ta Claus is com - in' to town. He's
naugh-ty and nice: San - ta Claus is com - in' to

7b

town. He sees you when you're sleep-ing, He knows when you're a -

mp

12

mf

- wake, He knows if you've been bad or good, So be good for good - ness'

16

f

sake. So, you bet-ter watch out, you bet-ter not cry, Bet-ter not pout, I'm

20

tell-ing you why: San - ta Claus is com - in' to town.

© 1934 (renewed 1962) EMI Feist Catalog Inc. and EMI United Partnership Ltd. This arrangement © 2015 EMI Feist Catalog Inc.
Reproduced by permission of Music Sales Ltd, Alfred Music Publishing Co., and Sony ATV Music Australia. All rights reserved.

ACCOMPANIMENT

• Part 1 uses G, A, B, and C on strings 2 and 3.

O little town of Bethlehem

Words by Phillips Brooks
Music English trad.

MELODY

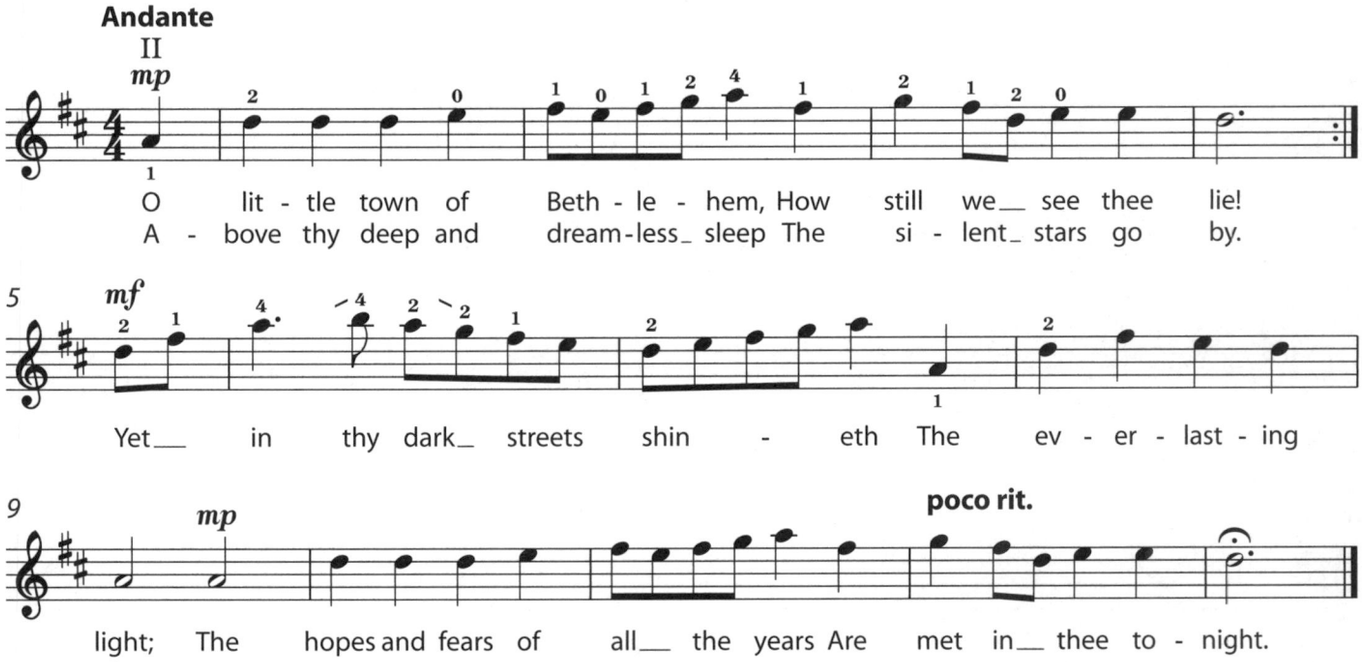

ACCOMPANIMENT

• Part 1 uses A, B, C♯, and D on strings 2 and 3.

© Oxford University Press 2015. Photocopying this copyright material is ILLEGAL.

Sleigh Ride

W. A. Mozart (1756–91)
(from *Three German Dances*, K.605)

MELODY

© Oxford University Press 2015. This page may be photocopied, but pages 30 and 31 may not.

ACCOMPANIMENT

• Part 1 uses G, A, B, C, and D on strings 2 and 3.

22
G7
C
F
C
mp (p)
mp (p)
mp (p)
2nd time D.C. (without repeat) al Coda
27
F
C
G7
C
G7
C
CODA
33
G
f
f
f
39
8va (opt.)
harm. 12
4
mp
mp
mp

CHORDS

Strummed chords can be added to many of the pieces in this book, by reading the chord symbols above ACCOMPANIMENT Part 1. Here are the corresponding chord boxes:

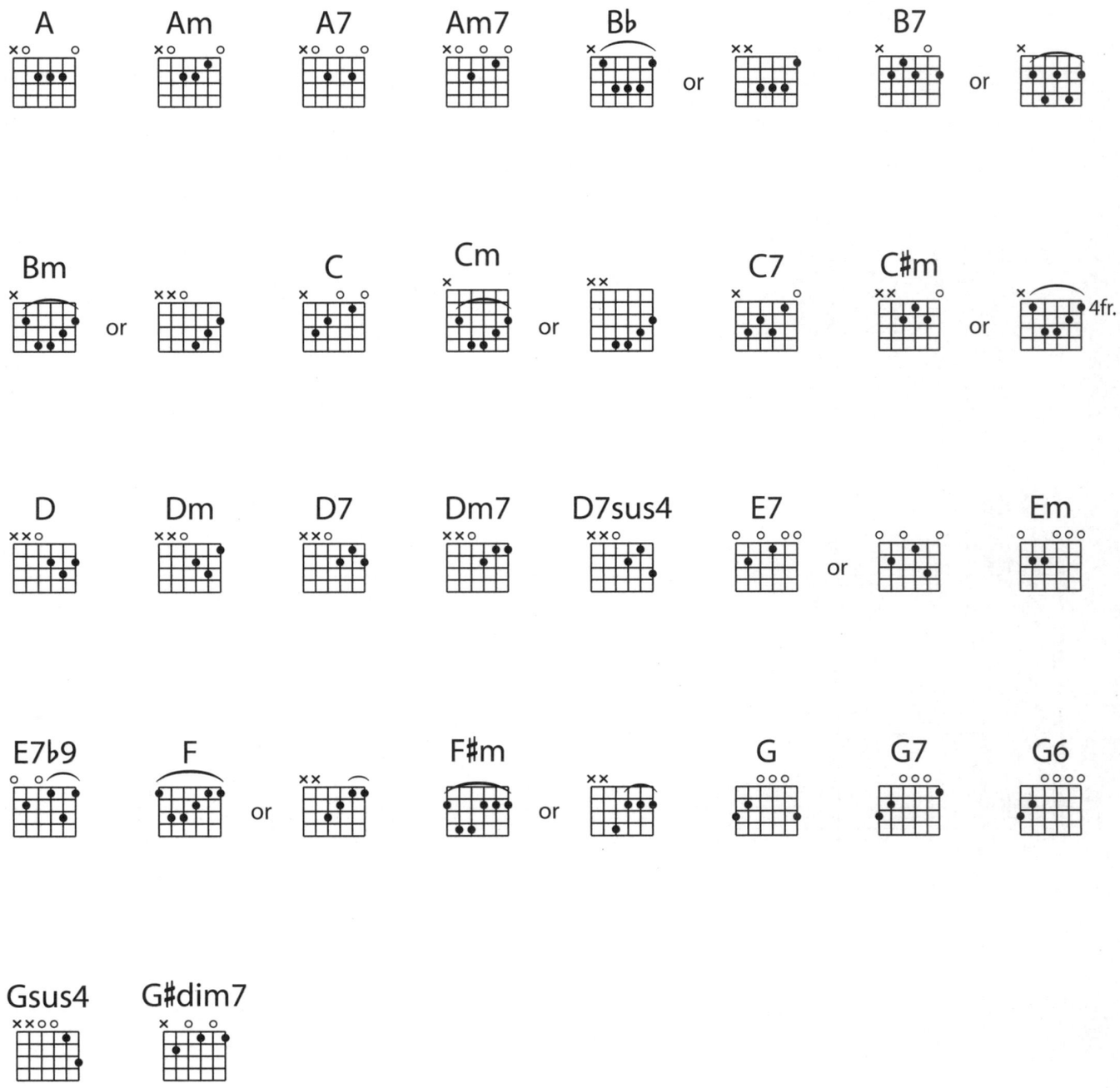